# That Day Will Not Come Except...

## 2 Thessalonians 2:3

Dr. Aaron B. Claxton, PhD

That Day Will Not Come Except… (2 Thessalonians 2:3)

Copyright © 2019 by Dr. Aaron B. Claxton, PhD

All rights reserved. No part of this book may be reproduced, stored in retrieval system, or transmitted in any form or by any means – electronic, mechanical, photocopy, recording, or otherwise – except for brief quotations in printed reviews, without written permission of the author.

Unless otherwise noted, Scripture is taken from The Holy Bible, The King James Version (KJV). The King James Version is in the public domain.

ISBN 978-1-947741-04-1

Kingdom Publishing, LLC
Odenton, MD 21113

Printed in the USA

# Acknowledgments

First and foremost, all glory, honor and praise belong to my great Lord and Savior, Jesus Christ. For He is worthy to be thanked for the strength, talent, ability, and knowledge of the Word which I have been given.

To my committed and faithful secretary, Elder Theresa Ward, who spent countless hours typing and retyping the manuscript when changes needed to be made, I thank you!

To my loving, devoted and accommodating wife, Dr. Deborah J. Claxton, who loves me, unconditionally. She has been patient with me even when I could have spent time with her and I used it to work on the book. Thank you, my Love!

To all of my Sons and Daughters, thank you for your love, your encouragement, and for blessing me for being your dad.

Thank you to everyone who at one time or another has sown into my life and encouraged me to record the words which I taught.

## Table of Contents

Chapter One - Discussing "That Day" ............................................... 1

Chapter Two - Identifying "That Day" .............................................. 5

Chapter Three - Two Major Events Before "That Day" .............. 9

Chapter Four - Counted Worthy to Escape, Go Through All  13

Chapter Five - Caught Up, Not Caught Away ............................... 15

Chapter Six - The 1000 Year Reign on Earth ................................ 17

Chapter Seven - The New Earth - The Eternal Home of the

Redeemed ............................................................... 19

Chapter Eight - Inheriting the Earth - God's Idea ....................... 25

*Chapter One*
# Discussing "That Day"

This <u>third</u> book on Christian eschatology is written in the same genre and spirit of our first two books—"The Biblical View of Rapture and the Second Coming", and "Caught Up to Meet Him".

Our basic premise, based on the Post-Tribulational and the Historic Pre-millennial positions of the Rapture and the Second coming, is <u>that these two events occur at the same time</u> and not seven years apart as the Dispensationalists and the Pre-Tribulationists so fervently insist-but <u>in error</u>!

Therefore, my aforementioned series of books are written to <u>correct</u> our Christian brother's errors, and to set the record straight, i.e., to *make straight the way of the Lord*; Thus, setting many misled believers free by presenting them with rightly divided Bible truth on this subject. To restate our premise we will state two postulations based in Bible truth:

At the Rapture, no one will be "left behind", because the church at this time does not go to heaven with Christ. <u>No, the church alive</u> on earth is <u>caught up to meet</u> Christ in the air, who is descending from heaven to earth with <u>"the dead in Christ"</u> <u>saints</u>. At that time Christ's destination is the <u>earth</u> where He will "judge and make war" along with His army of saints. (Rev. 19:11, 14-15.) First Thessalonians 4:16 says, *For the Lord himself shall descend from heaven with a shout…*That <u>shout</u> is described as the <u>war</u> <u>cry</u> of a Commander-in-Chief. Therefore Rev. 19:11 and I Thess.4:16 are <u>companion Scriptures</u> referring to the <u>same</u> event.

While speaking about premises allow me to point out that well known Christian eschatology teachers of the Dispensationist-Pretribulationist camp make the big mistake of calling the great tribulation the "wrath of God". Herein they are wrong, because the Bible declares that <u>the great tribulation</u> is in fact called "The wrath of Satan or of the devil" (Rev. 12:12). It says, *"Woe to the inhabitants of the earth and the sea! For the devil has come* down to you, <u>having great wrath</u>, because he knows he has a short time."

The wrath of Satan is unleashed upon the world and upon the saints through the <u>antichrist</u>; the beast who arises from the sea and is referenced in II Thess. 2:3b; Daniel 7:8, 21-22, 24-25; Rev. 11:7; 23:1-8.

Whether we are reading from Daniel 7 or Revelation 11 or 13, the beast's (antichrist's) reign of terror and persecution of God's saints will only last <u>3 ½ years</u>. Daniel records the following concerning the beast, i.e., the antichrist:

*He shall speak pompous words against the Most High and shall persecute (wear out) the saints, and the saints shall be given into his hand for a time and times and a half time (3 ½ years)* (Dan. 7:25). In Revelation 13:4-5, 7, we read the following, "Who is like the beast? *Who is able to make war with him? And he was given a mouth speaking great things and blasphemies, and he was given authority to continue forty two months (3 ½ years)… It was granted to him (by God) to make war with the saints and to overcome them (for 3 ½ years).* <u>But the antichrist's brutality against</u>

the saints (the great *tribulation, the devil's wrath*) will end with Christ's return."

Daniel describes this event as wise, *"The same horn (the antichrist) was making war against the saints and prevailing against them, until the Ancient of Days came…"* (Daniel 7:21-22a). The Apostle Paul describes the same events on this wise: *And you who are Troubled (enduring tribulation) rest with us when the Lord Jesus is revealed from heaven with His mighty angels in flaming fire taking vengeance on those…when He comes in that Day* (II Thess. 1:7-8, 10). Paul speaks more specifically of the man of sin (of lawlessness), the son of perdition (the antichrist) and the ending of his war against the saints when he says, *And then the lawless one will be revealed (out of the midst of lawlessness-not taken out of the way), whom the Lord (Jesus) will consume with the breath of His mouth and destroy with the brightness of His coming.* (II Thess. 2:8).

Beloveds, this is precisely the same scene that John depicts in Revelation 19:15 which says, *And the Armies in heaven…followed Him on white horses. Now out of His mouth goes a sharp two-edged sword…v.20, Then the beast was captured, and with him the false prophet…These two were cast alive into the lake of fire…*Thus the antichrist's 3 ½ yeas of great tribulation upon the saints is ended, and the wrath of God begins to be executed on the uprightness with the Second Coming of Christ!

Now to go to the base text of our book as found in II Thessalonians 2:3 which reads, *"Let no man deceive you by any means; For that day shall not come, except there come a falling away first and that man of sin be revealed the son of perdition."*

*Chapter Two*
# Identifying "That Day"

Let us immediately clarify which day that day is.

In verse two of II Thessalonians Chapter 2, Paul refers to the day of Christ; however in verse one, Paul defines and describes that day quite clearly. Therein Paul writes, *Now we beseech you, brethren, by the coming of our Lord Jesus Christ, and by our gathering together unto him…* That Day is the day of Christ's Second Coming, and the day of the Church's rapture or of meeting Him in the mid-air. Conclusion, this is one and the same day with no seven-year separation between them, and no trip up to heaven at this time.

I Thessalonians 4:15-17 demonstrates this same truth quite sufficiently. Verse 15 speaks of *the coming of the Lord…* And indeed that is the Second Coming of the Lord. And then verse 16 speaks of the living Christians (the church militant) being caught up together with the dead in Christ whose souls are descending from heaven with the Lord, so that the glorified bodies of both groups meet the Lord in the clouds in the air and remain with Him forever. From the mid-air, this one united church descends with Christ to His destination, to the earth, to judge and make war on His enemies, (Rev 19:11-19) and to reign with Him for one thousand years (Rev. 20:6).

## That Day Will Not Come Except

Again, the Day of Christ's coming and of the saints' gathering together unto Him (in the rapture) <u>cannot come</u> and <u>shall not come until the great apostasy</u>, or the <u>falling away from the faith</u> takes place. And this is happening now, even as we speak. And secondly, Paul said, *and the man of sin the son of perdition be revealed* (<u>out of the midst</u> of the great rebellion against God and <u>out of great deception</u>). Yes, we see this happening, especially in the area of homosexuality both inside and outside of the church. We see that pornography and all manner of sexual sin is rampant in the church today, and that the people would rather have it so! These ones are deceived by the antichrist spirit and will be deceived by the antichrist himself. Many will be lost, because *The coming (revealing) of the lawless one is according to the working of Satan, with ...lying wonders, and with <u>all unrighteous deception among those who perish, because they did not receive the love of the truth that they might be saved</u>. And for this reason, God will send them a strong delusion, that they should believe the lie, that they all may be condemned who did not believe the truth but had pleasure in unrighteousness (2 Thess. 2:8-12).* They will believe the lie that the antichrist is the True Christ—God manifest in the flesh.

*Whereas the <u>great tribulation</u> on God's saints for 3 ½ years reveals the wrath* of Satan against the church; it is the <u>Day of the Lord</u>, the Second Coming and the Rapture <u>that reveals the wrath of God</u> outpoured upon the wicked.

Paul tells us in 2 Thess. 1:6-8 that *it is a righteous thing with God to <u>repay with tribulation</u> (wrath and affliction) those who trouble you, and (for God) to give you who are troubled (being warred against by the antichrist)*

## Chapter Two - Identifying "That Day"

<u>*rest (relief)*</u> <u>*with us when the Lord Jesus is revealed from*</u> <u>*heaven*</u> *with his mighty angels in flaming fire taking vengeance (wrath) on those who do not know God…*

Therefore, we may truly say in light of numerous Scriptures we have examined in this writing, that the Second Coming of the Lord is a <u>rescue mission</u> for His saints on earth after the antichrist's 3 ½ years of brutality; and a <u>destruction mission</u> against the antichrist, the false prophet and their armies, according to Revelation 19:11-21. There the Lord descends from heaven riding a white horse and is followed by his armies of holy angels and saints (holy men and women) also riding white horses.

Note that before Christ's battle is joined with the antichrist and his armies, He pauses momentarily in the mid-air, so that the living saints on earth may be caught up to meet with the saints who have died in Christ, as their souls are descending from heaven with Him. After that <u>brief moment of mid-air meeting, reunion and glorification of our bodies, Christ then proceeds down with His host to earth to judge and make war on the antichrist and his host</u>. Jude combines that word with this word: *Behold the Lord comes with ten thousands of His saints to execute judgment on all…who are ungodly…* (Jude 1:14).

John wrote in Revelation 19:15, "*Now out of His mouth goes a sharp two-edged sword, that with it He should*

> *strike the nations...He Himself treads the winepress of the <u>fierceness</u> and <u>wrath</u> of <u>Almighty God</u>." Verse 19 says, "And saw the beast (the antichrist) the kings of the earth, and their armies gathered together to make war against Him who sat on the horse and against His army.*
>
> *Then the beast was captured, and... the false prophet. These two were cast alive into the lake of fire burning with brimstone. And the rest were killed with the sword which proceeded from the mouth of Him (same scene in 2 Thess. 2:8; Isa. 66:16-16) who sat on the horse... (vv 20-21).*

The portion cited above is a description of the events on the Day of the Lord's Second Coming, and the rapture of the Church.

*Chapter Three*
# Two Major Events Before "That Day"

Again from our base text 2 Thessalonians 2-3, we must conclude that <u>two major events must</u> take place before the Day of the Lord's Coming and the Rapture can take place. Those two events described in our base text are:

1. The great apostasy or falling away in the last days; and
2. The unveiling or revealing or coming forth of the Antichrist out of the midst of the spirit of lawlessness and rebellion in the world and in the church; <u>not the taking out of the way, as they erroneously say!</u>

Our book title is THAT DAY WILL NOT COME EXCEPT...<u>these two things take place first</u>. Therefore, the church will not and cannot make any <u>great escape</u> to heaven <u>before</u> the antichrist and the <u>great tribulation</u> come!

The dead in Christ (the church triumphant) will miss all of these events on earth. However, the living saints on earth (the church militant) will indeed face much tribulation and persecution as we have seen from the books of Daniel and Revelation.

Paul speaks of this in Acts 14:21b, and in Romans 8:17-18. Peter speaks of the same in 1 Peter 4:12-13. Let us return to our base Scripture 2 Thess. 2:3 once again to clarify another misconception that is troubling the church. Paul warned, *Let no* *man deceive you <u>by any means</u> (false letter, false prophecy, human reasoning etc.), for that day (Rapture and Second Coming) will not come unless the <u>falling away</u> comes first, and...*

For at least fifty years, the pre-tribulation teachers have foisted a "reinvented" meaning on the word <u>falling away</u> or <u>apostasy</u>. I was around when this error began to be introduced (eisegeted) into the Scriptures. They took the Greek word <u>apostasia</u> and forced <u>a physical or spatial departure</u> or <u>removal</u> (of the church) <u>from the earth</u> – in other words; that apostasy means "translation" to heaven.

Brethren, that <u>interpretation is as far wrong as the east is from the west</u>! What Paul meant by the <u>apostasy</u> or falling away is clearly seen in his prophecy on this subject in I Tim. 4:1. Let's read, *Now the Spirit <u>expressly</u> says <u>that in the latter times some will depart from the faith</u>, giving heed to deceiving spirits and doctrines of demons...*

Paul, in both of the above passages was warning the saints that in the end times the antichrist spirit of deception would be strong in the church causing some to <u>fall away from their faith in Christ</u> and to turn to false doctrines such as New Age, Islam, the love of money, illegal and perverted sex with impunity etc.; Paul indicated that out of this <u>deceptive environment</u> the <u>antichrist would arise, come forth or be revealed</u>.

Again, the King James Authorized Version gives us a <u>poor rendering</u> of II. Thess 2:7. The King James Version says, *For the mystery of lawlessness (iniquity) is already at work, only He (God) who now restrains will do so <u>until he is taken out of the way</u>.* That latter phrase in the Greek is <u>ginoma mesou</u>, which means <u>to arise out of, to be born out of or to be revealed out of the midst</u>. That expression is translated or rendered as such at least one hundred times in

Young's Analytical Concordance. We can safely say that the King James translators simply missed it on this one!

Therefore, all manner of concocted interpretations has come out of verse 7. Simply put, the antichrist will be revealed out of the midst of deception and lawlessness in the church and in the world. He will come on the scene as we have seen in Daniel 7 and Revelation 11, 12 and 13; and will wreak havoc upon the saints, the one New Man; the church militant, for 3 ½ years with God's permission, until Christ appears in the air with "the dead in Christ"!

Once the church militant is caught up to meet with them and all are glorified together, (Rom 8:17) then says Paul, *The Lord will consume (the antichrist) with the breath of His mouth and destroy him with the brightness of His coming.*

That's the long and short of it beloveds. We have been sold a bill of goods based on fear, sensationalism, human tradition and reasonings! But this third book in the series presents additional light on this subject to liberate our understanding from the doctrines and opinions of men.

*Chapter Four*
# Counted Worthy to Escape, Go Through All...

As we move toward the conclusion of this booklet, "THAT DAY WILL NOT COME EXCEPT…", there are two areas we must, of necessity, deal with. These areas are:

1. The so-called "great escape"; and
2. When the whole church goes to heaven.

Whereas we have probably touched on the above cited areas in two previous books on the Rapture and the Second Coming, it bears repeating and clarifying here.

Let's quote from Luke 21:36 which reads, *Watch therefore, and pray always that you may be <u>counted worthy to escape all these things</u> that will come to pass…* That passage sounds good, but, <u>other versions of the Bible read differently and with greater clarity and understanding.</u>

Before we quote that passage from other Bible versions, let us consider that the believers in Acts 5:41 rejoiced *that they were <u>counted worthy</u> to suffer for His name.* In II Thess. 1:4-5, Paul and others boasted about the patience and faith that that church was enduring in all their persecutions and tribulations which Paul called *manifest (plain) evidence of the <u>righteous judgement</u> of God <u>that you may be counted worthy of the kingdom of God for which you also suffer.</u>* In the Message Bible that latter passage reads: *All this trouble is a clear* *sign that <u>God has decided to make you fit for the Kingdom</u>.* In that same context Paul connected much or great tribulation on the believers <u>with entering the kingdom of God</u>. (Acts 14:22) Additionally Paul wrote, If *we suffer, we shall also, reign with him…Tribulation prepares us for God's Kingdom*!

Are you getting the picture? The word <u>escape</u> doesn't always mean to "flee out of". No, there are times that the word escape means <u>to go through danger unharmed</u>. The word escape has that very meaning in Exodus 10:5.

Again, Luke 21:36 in the Message Bible reads this way: *Pray constantly that you will <u>have strength</u> and wits <u>to make it through everything</u> that's coming…*

The Wycliffe Bible Commentary, p. 1063, on Luke 21:36 says, "An alternate manuscript reading, *<u>that ye might be strong enough to</u>*, is slightly preferable."

The Today's English Version of the Bible renders Luke 21-36 in a similar way as we saw above: *Be on watch and pray always that <u>you have strength to go safely through all these things</u> that will happen…*<u>These versions agree in spirit with</u> Paul's writings Yet (or yea) <u>in all these things</u> (tribulation, distress, persecutions, etc.) <u>we are more than conquerors through Him</u>… (Rom. 8:35-37). Paul insists <u>that we are more than conquerors by going through all these things</u> not <u>fleeing out of them</u>!

*Chapter Five*
# Caught Up, Not Caught Away

While we are on this point, allow me to show how my pre-tribulation brethren have forced an understanding and saying into the word of God which is simply not there.

They often talk about the Lord "catching us up" or "the catching up" or "the seizing" or the "snatching up" of the church by the Lord. To be <u>caught up</u> is <u>not to be caught away</u>!

What my pre-trib brethren have done is they have taken a quote from the Song of Solomon 2:10, 13 that says, *My beloved spoke and said to me: '<u>Arise</u> my love, my fair one, and <u>come away</u>',* and they injected a <u>prophetic meaning</u> into it, so that Paul's statement that says, *We shall be <u>caught up</u> together…<u>to meet</u> the Lord in the air,* became: *We shall be <u>caught away</u> with the Lord <u>to heaven</u>.* <u>This is the worst kind of eisegesis</u>!

Jesus made the following statement: *I will come again <u>and receive you to myself</u>* (John 14:3). He did not say he would come again <u>and take us to heaven</u>!

Our second point is when does the <u>whole church</u> go to heaven? <u>Especially</u> since the church currently exists in two realms- <u>heaven</u> ("the dead in Christ") and <u>earth</u>.

When Christ returns in the Rapture and the Second Coming, He brings the sleeping saints with Him whose bodies He resurrects <u>first</u>, and the living saints on earth are caught up to meet them in the air. After our momentary <u>glorification in the air</u> (I. Cor. 15:51-52; Col. 3:4; Phil 3:20-21) we continue with Christ in

His descent to the earth (I Thess. 4:16; II Thess. 1:10; Rev. 19-21).

## Chapter Six
# The 1000 Year Reign on Earth

After the scene depicted above, the Lord Jesus having put down: *All rule and all authority and power* (I Cor. 15:24), He begins His 1000-year reign (25). Rev. 20:6 says, *Blessed and holy is he who has part in the first resurrection. Over such the second death has no power, but they shall be priests of God and of Christ, and shall reign with Him a thousand years.* That reign is on the earth (Rev. 5:9-10b). After the thousand-year reign of Christ and the Church, Satan is released out of the bottomless pit where he has been imprisoned during Christ's earthly millennial reign (Rev. 20:1-3,7).

Satan proceeds to gather an army from the multitudes of deceived people on the earth and they surround the camp of the saints and the beloved city. *And fire came down from God out of heaven and devoured them* (Rev. 20:8-9). It is at this time that I perceive from Scripture that the whole church (the united Church) is caught up to heaven. It is here that I believe Isaiah's prophetic words in Isaiah 26;20-21 are fulfilled. His prophecy says, *Come, (to heaven) my people, enter your chambers, and shut your doors behind you; hide yourself, as it were, for a little moment, until the indignation is past. For behold the Lord comes out of His place (in heaven) to punish the inhabitants of the earth for their iniquity; the earth will also disclose her blood, and will not more cover her stain.* Once the glorified church, after the millennial reign, goes into God's presence in heaven and joins Him at the white throne judgement, we join in His judgment of those whose names are not found written in the Book of Life.

## That Day Will Not Come Except

(Rev. 20:11-15). Paul posed this question to the church in I Corinthians 6:2, *Do you not know that <u>the saints will judge the world</u>?*

After the present heaven and earth are <u>renovated by fire</u> (Rev. 20:11; II Pet. 3:10-12) we see the tabernacle of God with men, *and He will dwell with them and they shall be His people. God himself will be with them and be their God.* (Rev. 21:3)

My point and conclusion is that after the millennial reign of the church with Christ on earth, <u>we all</u> (the whole united church) <u>go up to heaven</u> to dwell with God. By the way, the biblical proof that the church will reign on earth with Christ is found in Revelation 5:9-10. It says essentially that the redeemed, as kings and priests to our God…*shall reign on earth.*

After the Church goes up to heaven John thrice records that the <u>Lamb's wife, the Church</u>, which is <u>the New Jerusalem, descends out of heaven from God</u> and <u>comes down to the new earth, our eternal home!</u> (Rev. 3:12b; 21:3, 9-10).

*Chapter Seven*
# The New Earth - The Eternal Home of the Redeemed

In this chapter, we take issue again with a popular notion, and the oft-stated expression: "heaven is my home".

No my beloved brothers and sisters in Christ, it was <u>not so from the beginning</u>! The Bible clearly shows us, when we believe and accept it, that <u>God's original intention was that He would rule heaven</u>, and <u>that mankind would rule the earth</u>!

In Isaiah 66:1 the Lord declares, *Heaven is my throne and earth is my foot stool*...So we may truthfully say that God rules in heaven upon His throne. But by the same token we see God commanding <u>mankind</u> (male and female) to <u>have dominion</u> and <u>to rule over the earth</u> and all its creatures therein, whether birds, beasts, fish, or creeping-things. <u>They were to rule over all</u>! Mankind was also told to be fruitful and multiply <u>via male and female co-habitation</u>, and to fill the earth with human beings. (Gen. 1:26-28) We are more than 7 billion persons in number at this time.

So, as surely as God declares that heaven is His domain, He also declares that the earth is mankind's domain, as seen above in Genesis 1:26-28. He further states this truth in Psalm 115:16, which says: <u>*The heaven, even the heavens are the Lord's; but the earth He has given to the children of men*</u>. <u>God's domain is heaven</u>, and <u>mankind's domain is the earth</u>! These truths were set forth by God as His original intention. The fall of man did not change God's plan. It is the same both now and forever!

Let's look at heaven and its purpose. When we read the Bible, God's revelation of Himself, his plans and His purposes, we see that Heaven is God's throne and dwelling place, and <u>the temporary dwelling place of the righteous dead.</u> (Isa. 66:1; II Cor. 5:8) The latter scripture referenced above says...*To be absent from the body is to be present with the Lord.*

Throughout Old Testament times God's dwelling place was heaven <u>and in the holy of holies.</u> <u>Jesus' body became God's earthly dwelling place for 3 ½-years.</u> Then, after Jesus died, rose again, ascended on high and sent back the Holy Spirit, <u>the body of Christ became God's earthly dwelling place</u> (Eph. 2:22), while the <u>third heaven continued to be God's dwelling place on high.</u>

After the renovation of heaven and earth by fire (II Peter 3:10-12; Rev. 20:11), John saw <u>a new heaven and new earth</u> (Rev. 21:1). John also saw God <u>dwelling literally in the midst of His people</u> and being their God in the New Jerusalem in heaven (Rev 21:3).

However, John also <u>saw the New Jerusalem and the Lamb's wife</u> (the church) <u>coming down</u> (descending) <u>out of heaven from God.</u> (Rev 21:2, 9b-10) Yes, the New Jerusalem (the church) will descend out of heaven and come down to the earth. The Bible says, *we* (the redeemed) *shall reign on the earth.* (Rev 5:9b-10)

And again, the word says, *<u>And the nations of those who are saved shall walk in its light</u>, and the <u>kings of the earth</u> bring <u>their glory and honor into it</u> (the holy city).* (Rev. 21:24) Surely, <u>according to God's rightly divided word</u>, the <u>renewed earth shall indeed be the eternal home of the saints!</u>

Listen to the unequivocal words of Jesus, the risen and glorified Lord: *Behold I am coming quickly! Hold fast what you have, that no one may take your crown. He who overcomes, I will make him a pillar in*

## Chapter Seven - The New Earth - The Eternal Home of the Redeemed

*the temple of my God, and he shall go out no more. I will write on him the name of my God and <u>the name of the city of My God, the New Jerusalem, which comes down out of heaven from my God</u>. And I will write on him, My new name* \*Rev 3:11-12). Please note that this is the Bible's <u>third testimony of the New Jerusalem descending out of heaven from God – no doubt to the earth</u>! The Bible says in several places, *In the mouth of two or three witnesses every word is established (as truth).* (II. Cor. 13:1, etc.)

The above cited truth is seldom heard in Christian circles today. Everybody talks about "going to heaven", and the righteous shall indeed go there <u>after the millennium</u> and <u>before the end of the Day of the Lord.</u> The Day of the Lord lasts 1,000 years (II Pet. 2:8). Isaiah describes that end of that Day on this wise: *Come, my people, enter your chambers, (in heaven) and shut your doors behind you, hide yourself, as it were for a little moment, until the indignation is past. For behold, the Lord comes out of His place (in heaven) to punish the inhabitants of the earth for their iniquity; the earth will also disclose her blood and will no more cover her stain (Isa. 26;20-21).*

Peter describes that Day and time this way: *But the day of the Lord will come as a thief in the night in which <u>the heavens will pass away</u> with a <u>great noise</u>, and the elements will melt with fervent heat; <u>both the earth and the works that are in it will be burned up</u>. (II Pet. 3:10)*

Let us remember here that the Day of the Lord <u>begins</u> with <u>Christ's Second Coming and the Rapture which take place at the same time</u>. After Christ subdues all rule, authority and power, he hands over the Kingdom to God the Father (I Cor. 15:24-28). But <u>Christ reigns</u> over God's Kingdom on earth for a <u>thousand years.</u> And we reign with Him. This is mankind ruling on earth. This is still during the Day of the Lord. Peter reminds us that with the

## That Day Will Not Come Except

Lord <u>one day is as a thousand years,</u> and <u>a thousand years as one day</u> (II Pet. 2:8). It is at <u>the end of the Day of the Lord</u> or the millennium about which John writes: *Then I saw a great white throne and Him who sat on it, <u>from whose face the earth and heaven fled away</u>. And there was no place found for them* (Rev. 20:11). This is the same scene reported by Peter previously. Both Peter and John saw a new heaven and a new earth after they were renovated by fire. (2 Pet. 3:13; Rev. 21:1).

Please note this beloved, the whole church of the redeemed are taken to heaven, <u>after</u> the millennium, but <u>before</u> God's indignation and fire are poured out on those two entities during His renovation of them. Jesus assures us, *Because you have kept my command to persevere* (in the faith), *I also will keep you from the hour of trial which shall come upon the whole world...* (Rev. 3:10). Yes, we will be protected in God's presence in the third heaven while His indignation is being outpoured on the earth and its unsaved, rebellious inhabitants. They shall be burned up with fire.

Once the renovation of the lower heavens and the earth are completed, then the New Jerusalem, the Lamb's wife, descends out of the third heaven from God to settle on the <u>new earth</u>. <u>From thence the redeemed shall rule the earth under Christ as God originally intended</u>. Then shall the "Lord's prayer" be answered and fulfilled, *Your kingdom come. Your will be done on earth as it is in heaven.* (Matt. 6:10).

The Wycliffe Bible Commentary, p. 1522 says, *That the Holy City comes down out of heaven seems to imply that it is not identical with heaven.*

Our vision and understanding of these end time events may not be perfect or without some flaw; <u>but we are reporting on these</u>

## Chapter Seven - The New Earth - The Eternal Home of the Redeemed

<u>biblical events as best we can based on the revelatory insight and premise that God gave us some fifty years ago.</u>  We don't profess to be all knowing, but <u>we do know what we know from the word of God which He has illuminated to our spiritual eyes.</u>

*Chapter Eight*
# Inheriting the Earth - God's Idea

The concept of a righteous people inheriting or possessing the earth is <u>God's idea</u>. This concept began to be expressed in Genesis 15:18 when God promised the <u>land of Canaan</u> (Rest) to Abraham and his seed or descendants. <u>Canaan was a microcosm of the whole earth</u> (Land of milk and honey). Adam, God's first son and heir, lost the inheritance of the earth when he disobeyed God and fell from grace. (Gen 3:1-7; St. Luke 4:5-8).

Jesus Christ through Abraham <u>replaced Adam as God's heir of the earth</u>. Matthew traces the genealogy of Jesus back to Abraham, and Luke traces it back to Adam. The apostle Paul calls Abraham *the heir of the world* in Romans 4:13, both he and *<u>his seed</u> through the righteousness of faith*. Beloveds, that's talking about you and me who have believed on the Lord Jesus Christ. <u>We are to inherit the world or the earth with blessed Abraham</u> (Gal. 3:9, 18, 29).

Again, the Bible speaks of Jesus Christ, *His (God's) Son, whom He has <u>appointed heir of all things</u>, through whom also He made the worlds (or the ages)* (Heb. 1:2). Jesus, who is the Word who was with God and was God (John 1:1) was in the form of God (Phil. 2:6). He originally existed in spirit form. He had to possess a flesh body in order to die for the sin of mankind (Adam) <u>and in order to legally become the heir of all things</u>. God the Father tells us in Revelation 21:7, He <u>*who overcomes*</u> *(the world and the devil, <u>by faith</u>, I*

*John 5:4; 2:14b) shall inherit all things, and I will be his God and He shall be my son.*

Please note that overcomers are placed in the same position as our Lord Jesus Christ who was appointed *heir to all things* (Heb 1:2). Is there any wonder that Paul calls believers in Christ, *heirs of God and joint* (equal) *heirs with Christ?* (Rom. 8:17)

What we are attempting to say is that God has not only given redeemed mankind the earth to be his eternal home; He has also made us His heirs and has given us the earth (the renewed earth) as our eternal possession or eternal inheritance! Nowhere does the Bible say that redeemed mankind is to inherit heaven. No! No! No! The truth about our inheritance or possession of the earth is woven throughout the entirety of the Bible, from Genesis (15:18) to Revelation (12:7). Psalm 37:9 says, *But those who wait on the Lord, they shall inherit the earth.* Verse 22 says, for *those blessed by Him shall inherit the earth*...Other Bible passages that echo this theme are: Ps. 25:13; Prov. 2:21; Isa. 57:13; 60:21; Matt. 5:5. As you can plainly see, this thread is woven throughout the Bible. The Lord really wants us to get His point! *The earth that is the Lord's and the fullness thereof* (Ps. 24:1), and it has been given to us the seed of Abraham because of our faith in Jesus Christ!

The earth that was made for mankind, was lost by man (Adam) and recovered by Man, (Jesus Christ) and will be handed back over to redeemed mankind, the Church!

I viewed a documentary on television recently entitled "The Kingdom of Heaven". Representatives of several major world religions were interviewed. Practically all of them expressed the view that heaven is mankind's highest goal. This motif is apparently present in most cultures of the world. But let us all be

## Chapter Eight - Inheriting the Earth - God's Idea

reminded that the Holy Bible is God's own revelation of Himself, His plans and His purposes! We have already noted that it is God's will and plan for redeemed mankind to inherit and possess the kingdom of the earth!

Psalm 2:8 reflects my statements above: *Ask of me, and I will give you the nations for your inheritance, and the ends of the earth for Your possession...* Here Christ is depicted as the Representative of redeemed mankind and the Son of David, the Warrior King. We see this prophecy being fulfilled in Revelation 19:11-21. In that biblical scene, we the redeemed of Christ are with Him.

We are certain that our insights in the word of God concerning the eternal home of the redeemed is shocking to some. Believe me, it is not our purpose to grieve anyone's heart, to smash long held precious views, nor to dash anyone's hope. Our purpose is to shed light on the truth of God's word, as I have been given to see it. Oftentimes we Christians fail to read a passage of Scripture in its fullness, and we therefore go on quoting just a part of that Scripture. Sometimes we build a doctrine on one incomplete state of a passage.

Allow me to cite an example. Deuteronomy 8:18 says, *You shall remember, it is the Lord your God who gives you power to get wealth, that He may establish His covenant...*(KJV). Most noted Christian Bible teachers quote the above passage and proceed to teach on "wealth to establish God's covenant" and for the most part that's where they stop. But that passage goes on to say...*His covenant which He swore unto our fathers as it is today.* The covenant which God swore unto Abraham in Genesis 22:16-17 says, *By myself I have sworn, says the Lord...*(the covenant repeated) *And your descendants shall possess the gate of their enemies...*The portion cited above is an addendum to the original covenant that God made with Abraham in Genesis 12,15 and 17. The above portion is called the oath. God himself identified the oath and the covenant as two distinctive parts of the same agreement. Hebrews 6:18 says, *that by two immutable things, in which it is impossible for God to lie..."* Those two things are the oath and the covenant; and in the oath the Lord specifically prophesied the transfer of wealth from the wicked to the righteous, saying; *and your descendants shall possess (seize or inherit) the gates (the power wealth and lands) of their (our) enemies* (Gen. 22:17; Prov. 22:13). This is the first documentation of this truth in the Bible.

Therefore, by many of our brethren sliding over this truth, they miss the source of where God promises that our wealth is coming from, which God promises to give us the power to get or obtain.

Some of the great Bible teachers have likewise failed to point out from the Bible that heaven is to be the temporary dwelling place of the righteous dead, and the redeemed, glorified saints. Because in the final completion of all things (Rev. 21:5), the New Jerusalem, the Lamb's wife, yea the Church, does not remain in heaven forever, but descends out of heaven from God (Rev. 3:12; 21:2, 9-10, and comes down to The New Earth-The Eternal Home of The Redeemed.

**BUT THAT DAY WILL NOT COME EXCEPT...**

# About the Author

Dr. Aaron B. Claxton has been in Christ for nearly 60 years and has preached the Gospel for nearly 60 years.

Dr. Claxton is the father of seven children, which initially and graciously began with his precious firstborn daughter, Gayle.

He has been married to his lovely wife, Deborah, for 60 years. They are the proud parents of six children (four boys and two girls), all have been called into the five-fold ministry. The Claxtons are also blessed with a host of grandchildren and great grandchildren.

Dr. Claxton's academic background includes earned degrees from Morgan State University, from the Mount Royal College of the Bible and from St. Mary's Semi-nary and University, where he pursued the academics for the Doctor of Ministry degree. He completed that degree in 1996 at the Family Bible Seminary.

Dr. Claxton has been awarded two honorary Doctorate degrees from Christian International University. They are the Doctor of Divinity and the Doctor of Laws degrees. He received his PhD degree in Biblical Studies from Family Bible Seminary in May 2003.

In addition to this prolific masterpiece, Dr. Claxton has authored over thirty (30) books of which nine (9) others are published (in addition to this one):

1 – "God's Plan for the Sons of Ham – a future and a hope"

2 – "The Biblical View of the Rapture and the Second Coming"
3 – "Farrakhan, Islam and Jesus the Messiah"
4 – "The Blessing of the Lord is Upon the Tither"
5 – "First Fruits the Missing Offering"
6 – "Possessing Our Earthly Inheritance Now!"
7 – "Caught Up to Meet Him"
8 – "Understanding the Root, the Causes and the Remedy of the Middle East Conflict"
9 – "ISIS – The Church's Wake Up Call"

Apostle Claxton, along with his wife, Deborah, founded and pastored the New Creation Christian Church in Baltimore, Maryland for twenty-three years. He has taught at three Bible Colleges and is well traveled, having preached the Gospel across America and in sixteen nations around the world.

Dr. Claxton stands in the offices of Apostle and Bishop, formally overseeing one hundred plus churches in the U.S., and in East and West Africa, and is presently being established in a global, apostolic ministry, along with his wife, Deborah, in her apostolic ministry. His oldest son, Apostle Aaron Bryan Claxton, along with his wife, Sheila, now pastor the headquarters church in Baltimore, which Dr. Claxton founded in 1968.

www.ingramcontent.com/pod-product-compliance
Lightning Source LLC
Chambersburg PA
CBHW050205130526
44591CB00034B/2155